Industrializing the
United States

Heather Price-Wright

Consultant

Jennifer M. Lopez, NBCT, M.S.Ed.
Teacher Specialist—History/Social Studies
Office of Curriculum & Instruction
Norfolk Public Schools

Publishing Credits

Rachelle Cracchiolo, M.S.Ed., *Publisher*

Conni Medina, M.A.Ed., *Editor in Chief*

Emily R. Smith, M.A.Ed., *Content Director*

Véronique Bos, *Creative Director*

Robin Erickson, *Art Director*

Michelle Jovin, M.A., *Associate Editor*

Lee Aucoin, *Senior Graphic Designer*

TCM Teacher Created Materials

5301 Oceanus Drive
Huntington Beach, CA 92649-1030
www.tcmpub.com
ISBN 978-1-4258-5062-3
© 2020 Teacher Created Materials, Inc.

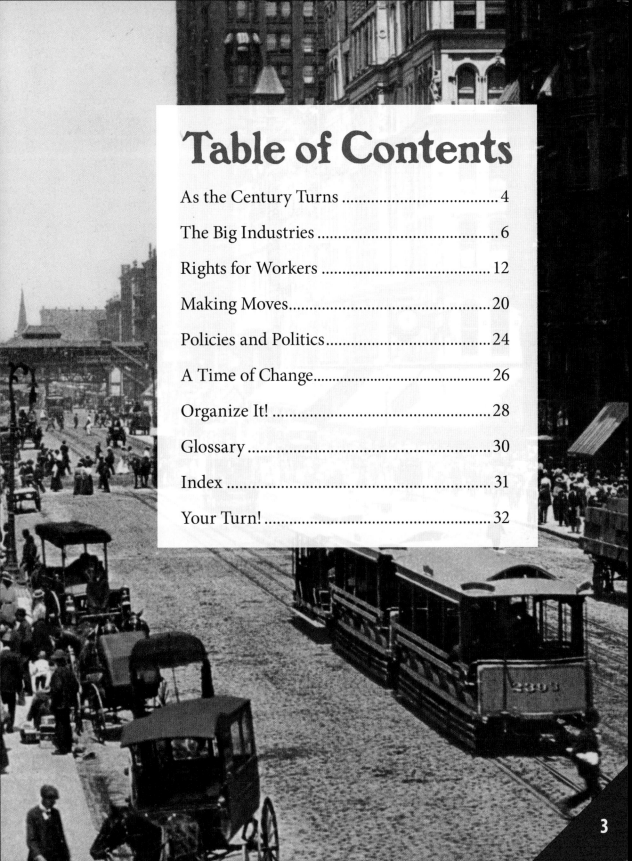

Table of Contents

As the Century Turns

The late nineteenth and early twentieth centuries were a time of great change in the United States. New technology changed how Americans worked. Machines and tools made it possible for people to work faster. Jobs moved out of people's homes and into large factories. This shift helped people in many ways. Goods were cheaper. Crops could be harvested at a faster rate, which meant more food for more people. New industries created jobs for people.

However, these changes had some negative consequences. Skills that helped people before were less useful. Instead of working with their hands, people were expected to learn how to operate machines. Working conditions were often bad. People worked long hours in small, hot spaces. Some children were expected to work dangerous jobs to help their families.

This period of change and growth reshaped the nation. People moved into cities to find jobs. The country as a whole was changing, and everyone was changing with it.

▲ A farmer uses a steam-powered tractor to plow his field in 1907.

City Living

After the Civil War ended in 1865, more and more people moved to cities to find work. The population of cities grew quickly. From 1870 to 1920, Pittsburgh's population grew from around 86,000 people to around 590,000 people! Chicago grew even faster as its population swelled to nine times its size during this period!

A Revolution

The First Industrial Revolution happened at the beginning of the nineteenth century. It took place mainly in Great Britain. British workers had new technologies and new skills. Over the years, these new skills and machines spread to other countries. They later reached Asia and the United States. This was the start of the Second Industrial Revolution.

New York City, around 1900

5

The Big Industries

A few industries led the charge in the United States' changing economy. There were major advances in how people traveled, built things, and bought goods. Leaders in these industries changed the way people lived and worked.

Make Way for the Model T

Automobiles first appeared in the late 1800s. But they were expensive and unreliable. Henry Ford and his Ford® Motor Company made cars available to average Americans. The Model T® was a Ford product. It was made from 1908 to 1927.

When the Model T was first released, it was very popular. People liked that it was both **durable** and affordable. Ford wanted to make Model T cars more quickly to keep up with the demand. So, he developed the moving **assembly line**. Each person focused on one task instead of doing the whole process. This technique is called *specialization*. It made production faster. The time it took to make a Model T dropped from 12 hours to less than 2 hours. Because of this, the cost of the car also dropped. When it was first released, the car cost $850 to buy. Near the end of its production, it cost less than $300. The cheaper price brought more customers. By the 1920s, Model T cars made up four-tenths of all cars sold in the United States.

Before Ford

In 1769, a French engineer named Nicolas-Joseph Cugnot was looking for a way to haul large weapons. He built a carriage with one wheel in the front and two wheels in the back. He used a steam engine to move the carriage. Many people consider this the first automobile.

A Study in Contrasts

Henry Ford was a complicated man. He had many **contradictory** views. He paid his workers $5 per day. That was twice as much as other companies in the automobile industry. He also shortened the workweek to 40 hours. However, Ford was also very controlling. He required workers to have neat homes. Men over the age of 22 had to be married to qualify for the $5-a-day wages. Ford also did not allow gambling, drinking alcohol, or other activities he disliked.

1900 photograph of a Model T moving through an assembly line

Henry Ford and his son stand by the first car Ford made and the fifteen millionth Model T made.

Riding the Rails

The first railroad to link the East Coast of the United States with the West Coast was completed in 1869. By the turn of the century, four more railroad lines crossed the country. These railroads offered more economic opportunities. People could easily travel to find better-paying jobs. Towns along the railroad lines grew. Parts of the country that had once been cut off now had access to goods from big cities.

In May 1894, workers at the Pullman Palace Car Company went on **strike**. They were protesting a pay cut. Across the country, other workers **boycotted** Pullman cars to show their support. By the end of June, more than 100,000 railroad workers had walked off the job. This brought many railroads to a halt.

President Grover Cleveland knew he had to act. Americans relied on railroads. He sent U.S. Army soldiers to Chicago, Illinois, where the strike had started. When the soldiers tried to stop the strike, the strikers fought back. A violent scene followed. Many people were afraid to strike after that. By the end of July, support for the strikers was almost gone. The trouble caused by the strike made many Americans turn against the workers and their **union**.

Mail on Rails

Trains began delivering mail in the 1830s. Mailbags were often thrown from moving trains. This method kept the train from having to stop at every station. Special devices called *catcher pouches* (shown above) were invented to smoothly drop off and pick up mail from moving trains.

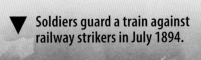
Soldiers guard a train against railway strikers in July 1894.

Union Organizer

Eugene Debs was an American **labor** leader. Debs was the president of the American Railway Union during the Pullman strike. He was sent to jail for six months for leading the strike. After he was released, Debs ran for president—and lost—five times. His fifth attempt came in 1920. At the time, Debs was in jail for speaking out against World War I. He campaigned from jail and received over one million votes.

A Nation Steels Itself

Steel production was one of the fastest-growing industries at this time. Steel is a strong metal that is made by combining two **elements**—iron and carbon. Early on, steel was hard to make and cost a lot to buy. However, in the 1850s, workers found a way of mass-producing steel. This method was called the Bessemer process. It used hot blasts of air to melt iron and make steel. Later, the open-hearth process proved to be more **efficient**. With this process, steel production grew quickly. In the 1870s, the United States was producing 380,000 tons of steel each year. By the 1920s, the country was producing 60 million tons of steel each year.

Goods for the Masses

Other inventions made life easier for people at home. By the 1870s, machines could spin yarn. They could cut and sew clothing. They could put together shoes and make nails. These were tasks that used to be done by hand in small shops and in homes. Now, these tasks were done in factories. Mass-production meant goods were less expensive. They were more widely available too. However, it also meant that many family-owned businesses could not compete and had to close.

tools for making shoes by hand

Steel is created using the Bessemer process.

Rights for Workers

Sudden economic growth came with downsides. Business and factory owners were often at odds with their employees. Railroads, steel mills, and other workplaces saw similar problems. This period was marked by some of the largest and bloodiest labor conflicts in U.S. history. These struggles shaped what it means to be a worker today.

Life in the Factories

Workers faced many challenges at the turn of the century. Work was often hard and dangerous. Machines made the work faster and easier. Factory owners did not need to hire skilled workers to operate the machines. Instead, these owners hired women and children, since they were only paid half as much as men were. Most people worked between 12 and 16 hours every day. They usually worked six days a week and had no vacations. Factory jobs were often dangerous. When workers were injured, they lost their jobs and had to pay their own medical bills. That forced many people to keep working even when they were hurt.

Despite the danger, the long hours, and the hard work, workers did not earn much money, and it was hard for them to make a living. Oftentimes, workers had to work more than one job to support themselves. Many workers thought their treatment was unfair. They wanted better lives.

Grave Danger

Factory work could be very unsafe. The only light came through windows. Smoke filled the air and made it hard to breathe. Machines did not have safety covers to prevent injuries. Machine operators could be as young as five years old. Tens of thousands of workers died from 1880 to 1900. Another 500,000 workers were badly injured.

Life in the South

During the late 1800s, many people began leaving jobs in farming to work in factories. Even though there were fewer farmers, new technologies meant that farmers could harvest more crops than ever. In fact, they could harvest more crops than the country needed. Farmers began selling crops to other countries. By 1900, U.S. farmers made one-fourth of their money by **exporting** crops.

1910 photograph of a young girl working in a cotton mill

Union Help

Workers began to form labor unions. These groups fought for rights. They wanted shorter workdays, higher pay, and safer jobs. When factory owners refused these demands, workers went on strike. There were thousands of strikes each year. Hundreds of thousands of workers took part.

These strikes often turned violent. One of the most violent strikes was the Haymarket Riot in 1886. Workers were protesting in Chicago, Illinois, to shorten their workdays to eight hours. Police were called in to watch the strikers. Suddenly, someone threw a bomb at police. Fifteen people died, including seven police officers. Many more people were hurt.

A bomb explodes at the Haymarket Riot in 1886. ▼

Eight men were arrested after the Haymarket Riot. There wasn't much proof linking them to the bombing. Still, they were **convicted**. Seven of the men were sentenced to death. The eighth man was sentenced to 15 years in prison. The Haymarket Riot was a huge setback for labor unions. Americans thought unions promoted violence. However, most union members were simply average workers fighting for better treatment.

▼ flier encouraging workers to protest in Haymarket Square in Chicago

Attention Workingmen!

GREAT
MASS-MEETING
TO-NIGHT, at 7.30 o'clock,
AT THE
HAYMARKET, Randolph St., Bet. Desplaines and Halsted.

Good Speakers will be present to denounce the latest atrocious act of the police, the shooting of our fellow-workmen yesterday afternoon.

THE EXECUTIVE COMMITTEE.

Achtung Arbeiter!

Große
Massen-Versammlung
Heute Abend, halb 8 Uhr, auf dem

Rebel Woman

The Haymarket Riot drew Emma Goldman to action. Goldman became a famous writer and speaker. She wrote about **anarchy**, women's rights, and antiwar beliefs. She was jailed many times for her beliefs. Eventually, she was sent back to her native Russia.

The Parsons

Lucy and Albert Parsons fought for workers' rights and for people's civil rights. Lucy was part American Indian, part African American, and part Mexican. Albert was white. Their marriage and their **activism** created many enemies. Even though Albert wasn't at the Haymarket Riot, he was found guilty of the bombing and hanged. After Albert's death, Lucy lived the rest of her life in poverty.

Save the Children

One major focus of unions was children's rights. At the time, about three in five children attended school. The rest had to work full time. Many families struggled to earn money. The average worker earned just 20 cents an hour. Everyone had to work to survive.

Children as young as four years old found work in factories. Factory owners wanted young workers. They could pay them less than adults. Children were also easier to manage. They didn't often join unions. Children worked between 12 and 18 hours each day. They worked six days in a row and were paid about $1 per week.

For many years, activists fought for laws to protect children from dangerous work. By 1900, there were 24 states with laws against children working in factories. People wanted a national child labor law. In 1924, Congress passed an act to make child labor illegal. However, not enough states **ratified** the act, so it failed to pass. Finally, in 1938, the Fair Labor Standards Act set strict age limits for workers. It said children older than 14 could work certain after-school jobs. Children could not work dangerous jobs until they turned 18 years old. The law also set a **minimum wage** for all workers.

President Woodrow Wilson signs a bill meant to discourage child labor in 1916.

▼ Young workers climb on machines to work in 1909.

A Persistent Problem

Today, many countries have laws against child labor. However, some people don't follow those rules. In 2012, the United Nations published a report. It said that there were about 168 million child workers worldwide. About half of those children work in dangerous jobs.

Workers' Holiday

Labor Day honors U.S. workers. It is observed each year on the first Monday in September. The first time it was celebrated was on September 5, 1882, in New York City. Twelve years later, Labor Day became a national holiday.

ABOLISH CHILD SLAVERY!

Women and Work

By 1900, about 1 in 15 married women worked outside the home. Almost half of single women held jobs at this time. These women earned about half as much as male workers. Women were also put in very dangerous situations at work.

Unions made life better for many workers. However, most unions would not allow women to join. Women had to form their own unions if they wanted to improve their working conditions. After years of working in harsh conditions, women began to stand up for themselves. Tens of thousands of women asked for laws to keep them safe. However, most people did not listen to their demands.

On March 25, 1911, the Triangle Shirtwaist Company's factory in New York City caught fire. Sadly, 146 workers died in the fire. Of those deaths, 123 were women. Most of the women who died were younger than 20 years old. The fire was so deadly because the workers were locked inside. Factory owners kept the doors locked so that workers would not steal items or take breaks. This tragedy forced the government to pass laws to keep workers safe. It also convinced many women to join unions and fight for better treatment.

Fighting Females

The Female Protective Union was established in 1850. This group worked to improve conditions for women in the **garment** industry. Women in this industry worked around 96 hours per week. They earned $2 each week. Unions helped improve conditions for working women.

Mother Jones

Mary "Mother" Jones was an Irish American labor leader. Jones convinced whole communities to strike along with workers. Unlike a lot of white activists at the time, Jones asked black workers to join her fights as well. Jones was once called "the most dangerous woman in America."

Firefighters fight the Triangle Shirtwaist Company's factory fire. ▶

Horse-drawn fire engines race to the factory fire.

Making Moves

In 1880, nearly half of American workers were farmers. Industrialization meant jobs moved from farms to factories. Eleven million people moved to **urban** areas around the turn of the century. These workers came from around the United States. They also came from other countries.

Many immigrants came to the United States to find work. In the mid-nineteenth century, a lot of immigrants came from Ireland and Germany. In the years that followed, people came from Italy, China, and eastern Europe. The majority of these people settled in big cities.

Life was not easy in big cities. The workweek was usually long and difficult. So people took advantage of the little free time that they had. They read books and spent time with other people. Communities gathered in churches, synagogues, and **saloons**. These places became important parts of city life. Homes were often cramped, dark, and hot. People didn't want to spend much time there. So they lived their lives in public instead.

Keeping in Touch

People were moving away from their home countries to work. But they wanted to stay connected to their families. Inventors came up with ways to help. Samuel Morse sent the first telegraph message in May 1844. In 1876, Alexander Graham Bell made the first telephone call. Railroads sped up mail delivery. Soon, it was much easier to share news across long distances.

What Did They Say?

Morse's first telegram was text from a Bible verse: "What hath God wrought." Bell's telephone call was a little less grand. Talking to his assistant, Thomas Watson, Bell said simply, "Mr. Watson, come here. I want to see you."

◀ New York City, around 1900

Life in Tenements

During this time, the population of cities grew rapidly. All these newcomers needed places to live. Since most people did not have cars, workers had to be able to walk to their jobs. That meant most factory workers lived in the same areas.

Cities were not prepared for the flood of people. There were not enough homes, which gave rise to tenement buildings. In these buildings, people—mostly immigrant families—were packed into tiny spaces. Each apartment was about the size of two parking spaces. Typically, apartments were joined together and did not have windows to let in light and fresh air. Many apartments did not have basic features, such as bathrooms. These buildings were often dark, dangerous, and dirty.

Wall Windows

According to New York law, all apartments had to have at least one window. Windows let fresh air flow through rooms. However, windows also cut down on the number of apartments that could fit inside a building. So, many tenement owners simply cut holes in walls. These "windows" opened into other rooms. In 1879, a new law was passed that said every room had to have a window that opened to the outside.

Eye-Opening Photos

Jacob Riis (REES) was a Danish-American photographer. He took photos of people living in tenement buildings. In 1890, he published these photos in his book, *How the Other Half Lives*. This book showed a wide audience what life was like in New York City's tenements. The book inspired new laws and forced Americans to take a closer look at how people were living.

▲ a family in a New York City tenement, around 1900

City governments couldn't keep up with the needs of the increased populations. The cities were often unclean and filled with smoke from factories. Still, people made the best of their conditions. Immigrants built thriving communities in the city. Their contributions helped define these cities to this day.

▼ Clotheslines hang between tenement buildings in New York City.

Policies and Politics

This time in history changed politics. Laborers lived tough lives and fought for their rights. At the same time, the leaders of major industries grew very rich. For them, this period was known as the Gilded Age. These leaders thought it was important to let companies, not governments, lead the way to a better nation.

The U.S. economy was also changing. People were relying more on credit. That meant they borrowed money from banks to make large purchases and then slowly paid it back. This system gave people more opportunities to buy new things. However, many people borrowed more money than they could pay back.

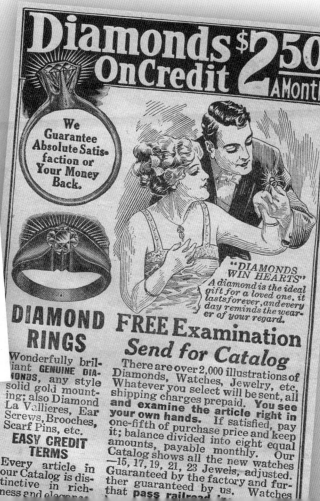

These ads encouraged people to buy things on credit.

People also began participating in the **stock market**. In the 1920s, stock prices soared. People believed that companies would continue to gain value. The period was known as the Roaring '20s.

Companies could not continue gaining value forever. People could not keep using credit. They had to pay back what they owed. All these issues reached a tipping point in 1929. The stock market crashed. The country was plunged into the Great Depression. It would take more than a decade for the United States to recover.

Turning a Phrase

Author Mark Twain coined the term "Gilded Age" to describe this period in the United States. When a person gilds something, they cover it with a thin layer of gold. Twain said this was like the United States. Some people were getting wealthy. However, these wealthy people concealed the poverty that most people faced.

The Progressive Era

In the late nineteenth century, many laws favored rich business owners over their workers. So, activists worked to change things. They led a charge to make politics less **corrupt**. This time was called the Progressive Era. It lasted from the 1890s to the 1920s.

▲ This political cartoon shows wealthy business owners being carried by their workers.

A Time of Change

A Changing Landscape

As families left areas in the countryside for cities, the landscape of the United States changed. By 1920, more Americans lived in cities than in the countryside. That had never happened before. It is still the case. Three out of four modern Americans live in cities.

Paying a Visit

The Tenement Museum is located on the Lower East Side in New York City. When people visit, they can see how families lived. They can tour the tiny apartments that families shared. They can even listen to recordings of people who lived in the buildings.

The Second Industrial Revolution was a time of change. Machines transformed how people worked. Many jobs could be done faster and easier than ever before. Companies became more efficient. Before, workers had to know every part of their jobs. However, specialization changed that. It made it so that workers only had to know one part of their jobs. They became experts on these parts. Business owners, including Henry Ford, proved that specialization was the best way forward.

There was a dark side to all that growth. People who worked by hand found it hard to find jobs. Machine operation could be dangerous. Many people had to work in harsh conditions. They worked long hours for low pay. Workers, including women and children, were treated unfairly. It would take labor unions and new laws to make things fair and safe for all workers.

The effects of the Second Industrial Revolution—both good and bad—changed the United States. Everything that happened next was based on the changing world of this time.

Children work in a factory in 1903. ▶

26

Chicago around 1890

Chicago around 1915

Organize It!

Early labor unions were successful when they chose specific goals and came up with plans to meet those goals. Imagine you are a factory worker during the Second Industrial Revolution. What working condition would you most want to change?

1. Working in a small group, come up with an action plan.

   > Why did you choose to address this problem?

   > How does this problem affect you? How does it affect your family and your community?

   > What form of protest will you use to change this problem?

   > How will you inform other people so they can be involved?

   > What community leaders or institutions can you turn to for support? What groups might oppose you? Why?

   > What will you do if your protest doesn't work?

2. After you have drafted an action plan, design a poster, picket sign, or handout that states what you're protesting and why. Your design should be clear and convincing.

WE only ask for Justice

▲ "Mother" Jones leads a strike in 1903.

Glossary

activism—the use of mass demonstrations for political purposes

anarchy—a state of confusion, lawlessness, and chaos

assembly line—an arrangement of equipment, machines, and workers in which work passes from one station to another until a product is assembled

boycotted—joined others in refusing to work with a group or a person to express disapproval and to force them to accept terms

contradictory—involving statements or beliefs that go against each other

convicted—found guilty of a crime

corrupt—dishonest or immoral

durable—staying in good condition over a long period of time

efficient—able to produce the desired results without wasting time, energy, or materials

elements—any of the basic substances that make up all matter in the universe

exporting—sending products to be sold in another country

garment—relating to clothing

labor—relating to workers

minimum wage—the least amount of money per hour that workers can be paid

ratified—made something official by signing it or voting for it

saloons—places where alcoholic drinks are served

stock market—a system for buying and selling ownership in some companies

strike—a period of time in which workers stop work to force an employer to agree to their terms

union—a group of workers formed to protect the interests and rights of its members

urban—relating to cities instead of the countryside

Index

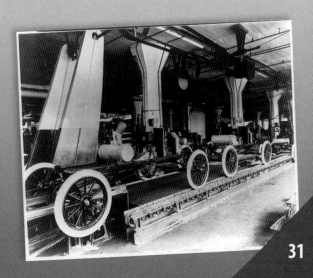

Your Turn!

Workers faced harsh conditions during the Second Industrial Revolution. Many people had to work for six days a week with no vacations. They often worked around 16 hours every day. Machines made work easier, but they made work more dangerous too.

Imagine you are the president of the United States at this time. You want workers to be kept safe and treated with respect. Write a list of rules that all business owners must follow. Be sure to include any rules about minimum wage, child labor, and injuries on the job. Design a sign that can be posted so that workers know their rights.